Virtual Assistance Mastery

Starting an In-Demand Remote Business Support Service

Table of Contents

Chapter 1. Introduction

Immerse yourself in the riveting world of Virtual Assistance Mastery with our Special Report, designed to help you harness the power of the in-demand remote business support service industry. This report is not about high-end tech jargons but real-life applications that can catapult your entrepreneurial journey with a successful virtual assistant business. If you've ever imagined swapping your nine-to-five grind for the flexibility of working from anywhere on your terms, your fantastic dream job doesn't have to remain a dream. Our Special Report is a comprehensive guide filled with practical insights, trends, success stories, and actionable steps that will help you design, launch, and scale a profitable virtual assistance business. Imagine being the cornerstone of someone's business, providing essential support while enjoying the freedom of remote work. Intrigued? It's time to master the art of virtual assistance and turn that energetic spark into a thriving digital business. Let's take this exciting and transformational journey together - your future self holding the reins of a competitive remote business will thank you!

Chapter 2. Discovering the World of Virtual Assistance

The realm of virtual assistance is an ever-expanding universe, with its own set of rules, expectations, and possibilities. As technology advances, so does the scope of what can be accomplished remotely, and the demand for virtual services continues to skyrocket. As you unravel the captivating world of virtual assistance, you'll find that it's a space filled with myriad opportunities, each tailored to your skills, interests, and personal aspirations.

2.1. Understanding Virtual Assistance

Virtual assistance (VA) involves providing administrative, creative, technical, or other business-support services from a remote location. This comprises a range of tasks, from managing emails and scheduling appointments, to handling social media accounts and undertaking market research. The beauty of this profession is its diversity. Each day as a VA is different from the last, with unique challenges, learning experiences, and rewarding outcomes.

Your workspace is not limited to a single location. With a reliable internet connection and requisite technology, your office can be just about anywhere - your home, a café, or even a beach thousands of miles away from your clients.

2.2. Skills Required for Virtual Assistance

While each VA role might require specific capabilities, certain key skills are universally vital.

Adaptability: The VA landscape is ever-changing, with new tools, platforms, and opportunities emerging regularly. Staying up-to-date with these will keep you competitive.

Communication: Effective communication is pivotal for building relationships with clients, understanding their needs, and delivering according to expectations.

Organizational Skills: Juggling multiple clients and tasks requires impeccable organization to ensure everything gets done in due time and to the desired quality.

Tech savvy: A decent understanding of essential productivity software, apps, and platforms is vital both for your tasks and for efficient communication.

Problem-solving: Since you are the support system for your clients, problem-solving skills will prove invaluable when you face challenges.

2.3. Opportunities in Virtual Assistance

The virtual assistance industry is booming and varied. Depending on your skill set, you might consider:

Administrative VA: You could handle traditional office duties like answering phones, managing calendars, and data entry.

Marketing VA: This involves tasks related to promotional activities, such as managing social media, creating content, and performing SEO.

Technical VA: If technology is your forte, you could handle website development, troubleshooting, and maintenance.

Financial VA: Budgeting, bookkeeping, and other financial tasks can fall to VAs with expertise in this field.

Remember, no path is etched in stone. You can always expand your services as you gain more skills and experience.

2.4. Establishing Your Business

Starting your VA business involves several key steps. You need to assess your skills, identify your niche, define your services, set up your rates, and market your skills.

Perform a self-assessment to understand where your strengths lie, and where you might need further training. Once this is done, determine the services you want to offer. You must also set competitive rates for your services. Too low, and you might undermine your skills; too high, and you may deter potential clients.

Starting a VA business requires some initial investment, such as a reliable computer and high-speed internet, secure data storage, and possibly website hosting and branding elements. Set out your business policies and contracts to protect both yourself and your clients.

2.5. Scaling Your Virtual Assistance Business

As your client base grows, so will your responsibilities. This is when effective time management comes into play. You'll also need to employ automation tools and software to handle increased demand efficiently.

To scale your business, you might consider adding team members or setting up an agency model. Remember, growth should always be manageable, and hastily adding new services or taking on too many clients can lead to overload.

2.6. Keeping Up with Industry Trends

Constant learning is a cornerstone of VA success. Stay informed about developments in technology, common software updates, and new platforms. Utilize online courses, webinars, podcasts, and books to stay ahead of the game.

The key takeaway is this: the world of virtual assistance is accessible, adaptable, and highly profitable for anyone with an entrepreneurial mindset, a penchant for diversity, and a readiness to learn and grow. Embrace this world's charm and unlock an ocean of opportunities.

Chapter 3. Branding Your Business: Making a Unique Identity

Starting a virtual assistant business hinges on more than just competency and good customer service. In today's saturated market, having a unique brand identity can set you apart and significantly contribute to your success. Branding is about creating a distinct image and perception in the minds of prospective clients that sets you apart from the competition.

3.1. Insights into Branding

Branding is not just about selecting a catchy name and a unique logo, although those are certainly part of it. It's a synergy of all the experiences, impressions, and interactions that your clients associate with your virtual assistant business. It encompasses everything from your visual identity (think logos, colors, and typefaces) to your tone of voice in communications and marketing efforts.

Your brand constantly communicates what you are offering and how it's different (and better) than your competition. It helps clients understand why they should choose you over other options, putting a spotlight on your unique selling point (USP).

3.2. Establishing Your Brand Identity

Establishing your brand identity is akin to embarking on a soul-searching journey. It involves defining the essence of your business and aligning all aspects of your business around that. Here are some steps to guide you through that journey:

1. Identify your vision: This is your big picture—the purpose behind starting this business. Your vision will guide all other aspects of your brand identity. Why did you become a virtual assistant? What do you hope to achieve?

2. Capture your mission: Unlike your vision, which is about your long-term goals, your mission reflects what you're doing each day to achieve that vision. It's the very essence of your offering.

3. Understand your value proposition: What do you provide to your clients that they value? What makes you stand out as a preferred choice? Clarify these to be able to articulate them consistently across channels.

4. Know your audience: To connect with your audience effectively, you need to know who they are. Try to understand their challenges, needs, and expectations.

5. Define your brand personality: Your brand personality should be a reflection of who you are—so that it comes across as authentic—and also appeal to your audience. If your target audience values professionalism and efficiency, your brand personality might be reliable and dedicated.

3.3. Building a Visual Identity

The visual components of your brand—logo, color palette, typography—are influential tools used in communicating your brand identity.

1. Start with your logo: This will be the most recognizable facet of your business. Make sure your logo design aligns with the overall personality and message you want your brand to convey. It should be distinctive enough to be memorable but simple enough to work in different formats and sizes.

2. Choose your color palette: Colors can significantly impact perceptions and emotions. The palette you choose should reflect the tone and ethos of your brand.

3. Select your typography: Fonts, like colors, communicate subtly. Font choices should coincide with your brand personality — for example, a tech-focused virtual assistant might opt for a modern, clean typeface.

3.4. Consistent Brand Messaging

The success of your brand hinges on the consistency of your messaging across all platforms and interactions. Equally important is your ability to communicate your value proposition effectively. Being clear and consistent in your messaging instills confidence and trust in potential clients. Develop a brand voice that reflects your personality and remains consistent whether you're writing an email or posting on social media.

3.5. Conclusion

In the end, remember that your branding is the first impression you make on potential clients. An effective brand motivates clients, fosters customer loyalty, and delivers the message clearly. By putting careful thought into the components of your brand, you are increasing your business's value and providing your team with direction. A strong, relatable brand identity can function as both a compass for your decisions and a magnet for clients.

Chapter 4. Essential Skills and Tools for a Virtual Assistant

Before we dive into the tools and skills necessary for a successful virtual assistant, it's crucial to underscore what a virtual assistant does. Essentially, a virtual assistant (VA) provides administrative, creative, technical, or specialized services to businesses, entrepreneurs, or busy professionals remotely. With remote work being the norm today, the demand for proficient VAs is continually increasing.

4.1. Personal skills needed for a successful VA

A VA wears many hats and balances multiple responsibilities efficiently. Thereby, a rich blend of personal skills proves indispensable.

1. **Reliability**: Above all else, a VA must be reliable. Your clients need to trust that you will deliver on time and maintain the high standard they expect.

2. **Strong communication skills**: As a VA, most of your interactions will be remote. Thus, your written and spoken communication must be clear, concise, and effective.

3. **Proactive approach**: Anticipating the needs of your clients and taking initiative shows your clients that you are genuinely invested in the success of their business.

4. **Time management skills**: Mastering the art of juggling your clients' tasks with precision is non-negotiable. You must learn how to prioritize tasks based on urgency and importance.

5. **Attention to detail**: Given the remote nature of your work, the margin for error is slim. A keen eye for the slightest inconsistencies is vital.

4.2. Technical skills for a VA

Depending on the services you provide, your technical skills may vary. However, certain fundamental technical skills underpin any VA's ability to perform their duties effectively:

1. **Proficiency with office software**: Knowledge of Microsoft Office suite or Google Workspace (formerly G Suite) is basic for any VA. These software tools help in accomplishing daily tasks efficiently.

2. **Social media management**: Many small businesses and entrepreneurs require assistance with managing their social media presence. Familiarity with platforms like Facebook, Instagram, Twitter, LinkedIn, and Pinterest is advantageous.

3. **Email management**: Efficient email management and understanding of popular email clients like Gmail or Outlook is also crucial.

4.3. Essential Tools for a VA

A successful VA and their tool kit are inseparable. It enables a VA to stay organized, communicate efficiently, manage tasks, and more. Here're some of them:

1. **Project Management Tools**: Tools such as Asana, Trello, and Basecamp help manage tasks in an organized manner.

2. **Communication Tools**: Slack, Google Meet, and Zoom are excellent platforms for remote communication.

3. **File Sharing Tools**: Google Drive, Dropbox, and OneDrive are perfect for sharing large files.

4. **Time Tracking Tools**: Tools like Toggl and Harvest help keep track of the hours you've worked for invoicing and productivity purposes.

5. **Email Management Tools**: Boomerang for Gmail and SaneBox are great for managing emails efficiently.

Virtual Assistance involves a myriad of services. Identify and master a niche catered to your skill set and see your business bloom. It could be graphic design, bookkeeping, content writing, social media management, or project management. Successful VAs continually upgrade their skills and stay updated on industry trends. The key lies in ongoing learning and adaptation to stay competitive and build a successful career as a VA. Armed with the right skills and tools, you are now ready to embark on your fascinating VA journey.

Chapter 5. Setting Up Your Virtual Office: The Basics

Before you can embark on your journey as a virtual assistant, the first critical step is setting up your virtual office. A well-equipped, organized, and efficient virtual office is the foundation for a successful venture.

5.1. Selecting the Right Technology and Tools

Finding the right tools is crucial to ensure smooth operation and communication within your virtual assistance business. A reliable laptop/PC and a secure, high-speed internet connection are the basics. Along with these, you might need productivity tools, communication software, and data management systems.

1. **Hardware**: A good-quality laptop or desktop machine is essential. It needs to have ample storage and a high-performance processor to handle online tasks without delays. Depending on the services you offer, other hardware requirements might include a printer, scanner, or webcam.

2. **Internet Connection**: A stable, high-speed internet connection is a must. Video calls, online meetings, and data transfers are standard in a virtual assistant role.

3. **Software**: Essential software for a virtual assistant includes word processors, spreadsheet software, graphic design tools, and email clients. Tools like Microsoft Office, Google Suite, or Apple's iWork provide all these functionalities.

4. **Communication Tools**: Tools such as Zoom, Google Meet, Microsoft Teams, Skype are essential for virtual meetings. Email and instant messaging apps will also be critical for daily

communication.

5. **Project Management software**: Some of the popular ones include Asana, Trello, or Basecamp. They help in tracking work and managing tasks efficiently.

6. **Data Management systems**: Reliable storage and encryption software are necessary to secure your client's data. You could use cloud storage options like Google Drive or Dropbox.

7. **Time Management Tools**: Tools like Clockify, Toggl, or RescueTime can be useful for time tracking and managing work hours.

By assembling this tech stack, you will have created a fully equipped workstation ready to cater to any client's needs.

5.2. Organizing Your Workspace

Once the tools are ready, the next step is designing your workspace. Opt for a quiet area in your home that allows you to work without disturbances. Make sure your workspace is comfortable and ergonomically set up. This will include a suitable desk, chair, and good lighting.

It is important to keep all your equipment within easy reach to ensure that you can quickly access anything you need without breaking your workflow. This could be filing cabinets for paper documents, shelves for binders and books, or organizers for your cables and other peripherals.

One of the keys to a successful virtual office is organization. Create a system for managing your tasks, time, and client files. You might consider using software like Evernote for note-taking and organizing information, or a physical filing system that allows you to keep track of paper files.

5.3. Building Effective Communication Channels

Communication is the cornerstone of a successful virtual assistance business.

Remote work often requires more communication than traditional office environments. Design a communication plan to ensure you stay updated with clients and manage projects efficiently. This would involve regular check-ins via emails or video calls, updating the work progress on project management software, and immediate communication about any challenges or delays.

Choose a platform that works best for you and your clients. Be it Slack, Teams, Telegram, or any other method, ensure that the platform allows for seamless information exchange.

5.4. Setting up Professional Services

With a professional look and feel to your services, you are sure to impress your clients right from the start. This can be achieved by setting up a professional-looking email address, preferably with your domain name. Using an invoicing and billing system also adds to your professional image and facilitates smoother business transactions.

5.5. Knowing The Legalities

It's crucial to understand the legal implications when you're setting up your virtual assistant business. Issues such as privacy, data security, contracts, and business registration are just a few things you may need to consider. Depending on your location, hiring a local business lawyer for advice would be optimal.

With your virtual office set up, you're now ready to embark on your journey as a professional virtual assistant. Remember, while setting up the office is a crucial step, keeping it organized and upgrading your tools periodically is equally important to ensure the smooth running of your business. The next steps involve marketing your business, honing your skills, and finding clients, but with a well-equipped virtual office, you've already taken the first big step towards starting your successful virtual assistant business.

Chapter 6. Winning Clients: Marketing and Networking Strategies

Every successful business venture starts with winning clients. In this journey, you will need to effectively market your services and build a robust professional network to solidify your client base. This exhaustive guide will help you navigate through the various steps and strategies needed to attract potential clients to your virtual assistance business. Let's dive in!

6.1. Develop Your Unique Selling Proposition

Before you start reaching out to potential clients, you need to understand your unique selling proposition (USP). What sets you apart from other virtual assistants? Reflect on your strengths, skills, and areas where you can specialize. This could be anything from proficiency in a second language, experience in a particular industry, or expertise in a unique business tool or software.

Your USP should run like a vein throughout your marketing content. It will make you more memorable to prospective clients. Make sure to highlight it during client meetings and conversations, in your website copy, and on your social media bios.

6.2. Build a Strong Online Presence

In the digital era, an online presence is essential. It's often the first point of contact between you and prospective clients. Your digital identity needs to present your skills, experience, USP, and work ethic convincingly to appeal to potential clients.

- **Website**: Your website is your digital home base. It should be professional-looking, easy to navigate, and provide clear information about the services you offer. Showcase your case studies, client testimonials, and portfolio here. Don't forget to use SEO strategies to make your website more discoverable to potential customers.

- **Social Media**: LinkedIn is an essential platform for B2B networking. Create a compelling LinkedIn profile where you outline your skills, experience, and the unique services you offer. Other platforms like Twitter, Facebook, and Instagram can also be useful depending on your potential clients' preferred online regions.

- **Content Marketing**: Sharing useful and relevant content solidifies your authority within your niche. Blog posts, infographics, videos, white papers, and case studies all make excellent content marketing materials. They help demonstrate your expertise and bring more visibility to your brand.

6.3. Networking

Networking is an essential component of any marketing strategy. The power of personal relationships and connections cannot be understated. Here's how you can start:

- **Online networking**: Join LinkedIn and Facebook groups relevant to your niche. Actively engage in discussions, share your expertise, and start building relationships. You can also attend virtual industry conferences and webinars.

- **Offline networking**: Attend local business events and workshops. You never know where you might meet a potential client or referral source.

6.4. Email Marketing

Email marketing remains one of the most effective forms of digital marketing. Building an email list of people interested in your services allows you to engage with them at their convenience. Consistently sharing helpful tips, industry insights, and updates about your services will keep you at the top of their mind when they need a virtual assistant.

6.5. Partnership and Collaborations

Partnering with other professionals whose services complement yours can be an excellent way to gain referrals. For example, if you specialize in social media management, you could partner with a website designer or an SEO expert. They might refer clients who need your services, and you can do the same for them in return.

6.6. Asking for Referrals

Don't hesitate to ask your happy clients for referrals. If they're pleased with your services, they'd probably be happy to spread the word. Offer a small incentive like a discount on next month's services if a referral leads to a new client.

6.7. Keep Continually Learning and Updating Your Skills

The virtual assistance industry is incredibly dynamic, with new tools and techniques emerging regularly. Invest in your personal and professional development by learning new skills, taking courses, or earning certifications within your niche. As a virtual assistant, you're a valuable resource to your clients, and the more you know, the more you can offer them.

Remember, winning clients is not an overnight task. You need to be persistent, strategic, and patient. Trust the process, maintain your productivity, and soon, you'll see your business flourish. With these strategies, you are better equipped to land your first, tenth, or hundredth client. The world is your oyster; you just need to know how to seize the opportunities.

Chapter 7. Crafting Effective Service Packages

Before embarking on the journey to craft irresistible service packages, it is vital to understand that your package is not just a collection of tasks you carry out. It is a holistic experience designed to solve your client's problems and offer them immense value. Creating a suite of packages that cater to diverse clients and their varied needs can be challenging yet rewarding, guaranteeing a competitive edge in the robust virtual assistance marketplace.

7.1. Identifying Your Clientele

Understanding your target audience is the cornerstone of a prolific service package. It's not about who you want to work with but about who needs your expertise.

Begin by defining your ideal clients. Are they entrepreneurs, small business owners, freelancers, or large corporations? A clear picture of your clientele will help to demystify their problems, expectations, and what they value most. Consider their industries, company size, operational challenges, and future plans. The more specific you get, the easier it will define a package tailored to their requirements.

With a thorough understanding of your clientele, dive deeper into the pain points. These are obstacles your targeted clients are facing, hampering their growth or productivity. Your role as a virtual assistant lies in addressing these pain points and propelling your clients towards success.

7.2. Defining Your Services

Having acknowledged your clientele's needs, now step into honing your service spectrum. The services you deliver are a reflection of your skills, interests, and market demand, collectively aimed at resolving client pain points.

List all potential services you could provide, from administrative tasks like email management, scheduling, to specialized activities like social media management, SEO, content writing, etc. Further, conduct market research to determine which of these services are currently in demand and align well with your abilities.

Evaluate these services, keeping in view your expertise, client needs, and market trends. Ensure you are knowledgeable, comfortable, and efficient in delivering those tasks. This will help your clients perceive your brand as reliable.

7.3. Structuring Your Packages

Now, it's time to shape-up your service packages. Start by grouping related services. For instance, blog management could couple with SEO optimization and social media promotion. This approach simplifies the selection process for clients and provides a comprehensive solution.

Next, consider the scope of work in each package. Offering various levels - for instance, basic, intermediate, and advanced packages, caters to businesses of all sizes. However, be transparent about what each package includes to prevent future misunderstandings.

7.4. Pricing Your Packages

Pricing can be a real balancing act. It needs to reflect the value you provide, the market rate, and still attract clients. Some virtual assistants base their rates on an hourly model. However, packaging your services allows you to break the time-for-money cycle and demands your price based on value rather than hours.

Conduct thorough research to understand the ongoing rate for services similar to yours. Set your prices, considering your expertise, the perceived value of your services, the demand, and the results you deliver. An adequately priced package should cover your expenses, generate profit, and justify the value delivered.

7.5. Marketing Your Packages

Successfully marketing your services builds the bridge between you and your clients. Start with clear, compelling descriptions of each package, articulating what's included and the benefits.

Leverage your website and social media platforms to promote your packages. Innovative, engaging content grabs attention, piques curiosity, and exhorts the viewer to explore more about your services.

Using client testimonials, case studies, and success stories fortifies your credibility. Alignment of these promotional tactics with your overall marketing strategy will yield a positive growth trajectory for your virtual assistant business.

7.6. Fine-tuning and Adapting

Stay alert to the dynamic market trends and alter your packages accordingly. Request feedback from your clients periodically to understand if your services are hitting the mark. If not, analyze and rectify. Remember, your package is fluid and requires constant adjustments, keeping in sync with the evolving industry.

Embrace the iterative nature of the process. You might not get everything right the first time. Minor adjustments along the way will provide valuable insights, leading you closer to crafting the impeccable service package.

Mastering the crafting of effective service packages paves the way for a flourishing virtual assistance practice. Your well-curated packages will not just help you stand out, but more importantly, become an invaluable asset for your clientele. Embark on this exciting adventure to create, refine, and perfect your offering, and witness your virtual assistant business skyrocket.

Chapter 8. Managing Client Expectations and Building Relationships

Managing client expectations and building solid relationships is an instrumental aspect of a successful Virtual Assistance business. This task is multifaceted, involving clear communication, setting realistic goals, maintaining consistent quality, and investing in relationships to retain long-term clients.

8.1. Understanding Client Needs

Mutual understanding forms the bedrock of managing expectations. Invest time in comprehending the strategic objectives of your clients, their working style, the technology they operate with, and their key motivation triggers. This includes understanding:

- The client's business model and operations

- The nature and scope of the tasks they intend to delegate

- Their overarching strategic goals and how your assistance fits into this

A comprehensive Client Needs Analysis can help you gather these insights. It should cover everything from communication preferences, specific skill requirements, project urgencies, to confidentiality arrangements.

8.2. Setting Realistic Expectations

One common pitfall in the role of a Virtual Assistant is over-promising and under-delivering. Be honest about your capabilities, your time commitment, and your skill set. Do not promise something you cannot deliver. Consistently under-delivering will lead to disappointed clients and can damage both your business relationships and your reputation as a service provider.

Create a Service Level Agreement (SLA) that clearly communicates:

- The tasks you will handle
- The quality and quantity of work to be done
- The time frame for completion
- What the clients can expect in terms of outcomes

An SLA will ensure that you're not overstepping your boundaries and the client will have a benchmark to measure your performance.

8.3. Effective Communication

The success of your client relationships will largely depend on how effectively you communicate. Clarity, openness, and diplomacy should be the tenets of your client communication strategy. Regular dialogue is necessary to address:

1. Work standings
2. Problems encountered
3. Potential changes in strategy or direction
4. Deadlines and deliverables

Moreover, it's advisable to tailor your communication to match the client's style and preferences. Keep it professional, concise, and timely.

8.4. Feedback and Improvement

Constructive feedback is valuable for enhancement of your services, and for learning and growing as a professional. Encourage your clients to provide feedback, and be open and responsive to their suggestions or complaints. A well-fitted reconciliation and appeasement strategy should be an intrinsic part of your customer service policy.

Proactively improve and adapt your services and workflows based on the feedback - showing the client you value their input and are working towards betterment.

8.5. Building and Nurturing Relationships

Virtual Assistance is not about one-time transactions, it's about long-term relationships. Establishing a human connection with your clients beyond just business can bring in trust, loyalty and repeated assignments. This could involve celebrating their successes, understanding their challenges, empathizing with their struggles and merely 'being there' when they need support.

The recipe for fostering strong client relationships includes:

- Regular Check-ins: Keep the lines of communication open and have regular check-ins beyond work discussions.

- Empathy: Put yourself in the client's shoes to understand their perspectives and challenges.

- Dependability: Show consistency in quality and timelines to reinforce their trust in you.

- Respect: Treat the client's time, business, and needs with respect.

In conclusion, managing client expectations and building

relationships are critical for the survival and escalation of your Virtual Assistance business. It takes both strategic thinking and emotional intelligence to build these relationships. Demonstrating your reliability through meeting expectations, maintaining open communication, incorporating feedback, and nurturing the relationship will go a long way in fostering lifelong clients who can catalyze your Virtual Assistance empire.

Chapter 9. Mastering Time Management and Productivity

In the world of virtual assistance, productivity and time management aren't just important - they're essential. In this competitive industry, efficiency and precision can make the difference between finding success and getting lost in the shuffle. As this journey unfolds, there will be a multitude of tasks requiring your attention. The challenge lies not only in completing these tasks but managing your time effectively to fulfil them without feeling overwhelmed.

Let's start by understanding time and its management.

9.1. The Essence of Time Management

Time management is the art of planning and controlling how much time to spend on specific activities. It's a skill that can be beneficial in all aspects of life, not just for a virtual assistant. Good time management leads to improved efficiency and productivity, less stress, and better chances of career success.

There are no shortcuts to it. You cannot manage time – we all have the same 24 hours in a day. The key is to manage ourselves within the time we have. It's about setting clear priorities, focusing on the tasks at hand, and organizing our work effectively.

9.2. Understanding the Value of Time

In any profession, understanding the value of time is paramount. As the old saying goes, "time is money." But in the world of a virtual assistant, time is more than just money. It is about building a reputation, establishing credibility, and becoming the most reliable professional out there.

The critical takeaway here is to realize that time is a finite resource - one that you can never get back. No amount of money can buy time. Thus, it is critical for every virtual assistant to utilize every single minute wisely.

9.3. Essential Time Management Skills

Certain skills can make you different from other virtual assistants - making you more productive, efficient, and stress-free. Here are some of these skills worth developing:

1. Prioritization: The ability to see what tasks are more critical than others is an invaluable skill. Knowing which jobs to tackle first and which can wait will have a substantial impact on your productivity and work quality.

2. Planning: Planning out your day, week, or even month in advance will save you a lot of time and prevent any unexpected surprises.

3. Setting Goals: Goal setting not only gives you a direction but also acts as motivation. Setting short term, medium-term, and long term goals and working towards them will greatly enhance your productivity.

4. Delegation: You cannot do everything yourself; it is more productive to delegate tasks when possible.

9.4. Productivity in Practice

Productivity is often misconstrued as just getting more work done, but this isn't entirely correct. Productivity is a measure of the efficiency of a person completing a task. If you finish a task efficiently and well, that means you've been productive.

Here are some well-proven productivity methods to enhance your work:

1. The Pomodoro Technique: This time management trick encourages people to work within the time they have rather than battling against it.

2. The 2-Minute Rule: If a new task comes in and it can be done in two minutes or less, do it right away.

3. The Eisenhower Box: This method provides a way to consider and organize tasks by urgency and importance. It can help you focus on long-term goals while navigating short-term needs.

4. Time Blocking: By scheduling blocks of time for different tasks, you'll eliminate the need to multi-task and increase focus, making your work more efficient.

9.5. Making Time Management and Productivity Habits

Building good habits is fundamental to becoming a master at time management and productivity. Even the smallest changes in habits can lead to significant impacts on your productivity and can considerably decrease the time you spend on activities without affecting the quality of your work.

Practices like breaking down tasks into manageable chunks, tracking your time spent on different tasks, limiting distractions, not being a perfectionist and setting realistic goals can be very helpful.

Remember, this is a continual process. You might not observe the benefits initially, but do not waver. Over time, you will notice the compound effects of these small changes leading to more significant improvements.

9.6. Tools and Technology

Technology plays an essential role in improving time management and productivity. Various software and applications are available to help you organize, set priorities, offer reminders, and generally streamline your work process. Examples include Trello, Asana, Google Calendar, Rescue Time, and several others.

By mastering your time management and productivity, not only will you become more successful in your virtual assistant role, but you'll also find more time to enjoy life outside work. This isn't just about improving your professional life - it's about crafting a better, more efficient, and fulfilling path for yourself. Focus, strategize, make changes, and implement - your path to Virtual Assistance Mastery awaits!

Remember, your journey as a virtual assistant is not a sprint – it's a marathon. Equip yourself well, and stay steady. And in this ride, your ability to manage time effectively and work productively are your best aides. Practice and make the best use of these tips. Embrace these tools and techniques, recognize what works best for you, and you will be well on your way to building a successful career as a virtual assistant!

Chapter 10. Scaling Your Business and Utilizing Outsourcing

As your virtual assistance business grows, it's crucial to ensure your operations can sustain an increasing workload. In the initial stages, you may have been able to manage all clients and tasks effectively by yourself. However, as you acquire more customers, it might become challenging to keep up with all their needs single-handedly. This stage calls for scaling your business and considering outsourcing as a method to keep up with the growing demands.

10.1. Building Systems and Processes

First, you need to streamline your business operations. Having systems and processes in place isn't only for corporations; even small businesses need these tools to function effectively as their client base grows. As a virtual assistant, you'll need to create systems for managing tasks, communication, payments, and customer support.

Invest in a robust project management system where you can track project progress, due dates, and manage different client tasks in one place. Some popular tools include Asana, Trello, and Monday.

Implement a centralized communication system such as Slack or Microsoft Teams. This platform will serve as your virtual office where you can interact with your clients and team.

Automatic invoicing software like Quickbooks or Freshbooks will be needed to keep track of payments and send out invoices without manually having to create each one.

Lastly, providing excellent customer support is paramount. Using ticketing systems like Zendesk or Intercom can help manage customer issues and ensure their needs are met promptly.

10.2. Hiring the Right People

Your team is the backbone of your VA business. You need to hire the right people who can represent your business effectively.

Begin by identifying the key roles you need in your team. You'll likely need more VAs to assist with the increasing workload. But you might also need a project manager, marketing specialist, customer service representative, etc.

Screen potentials hires thoroughly. Consider their expertise, work ethic, and reliability. Also, consider their time zone and availability to ensure they can effectively serve your client base.

To find this talent, you can use recruitment platforms such as LinkedIn, freelance platforms like Upwork or Fiverr, or VA-specific recruitment agencies.

10.3. Training Your Team

Once you have assembled your team, the next step is to ensure they are skilled enough to deliver your promises to your clients. This means setting up a comprehensive training program.

Your training program should educate your team on their respective roles, your business values, clients' needs, and expectations, and how to use the business's various systems and processes. The goal is to create a competent and independent team that can handle tasks even when you're not directly supervising them.

10.4. Outsourcing to Other VAs

As your business expands, your responsibilities increase, and time becomes a scarce commodity. This is where outsourcing becomes crucial. And who better to understand your needs than another VA business?

Outsourcing to other VAs or VA agencies can offer several benefits. It provides the advantage of professional services without hiring full-time employees. A VA agency can also offer specific services that may be out of your expertise but required by your clients.

However, in outsourcing, it's vital to maintain your brand's consistency. Ensure the services you outsource adapt to your business's existing norms and standards to provide a cohesive experience for your clients.

10.5. Monitoring and Assessment

Growth comes with new challenges. It's crucial to regularly evaluate your operations to ensure your systems, processes, and team are functioning optimally. Make use of data analytics tools to monitor your business's performance. Regularly seek feedback from your clients and team to identify areas of improvement.

Scaling your business and utilizing outsourcing is an exciting journey! It may be challenging, but the rewards are worthwhile. Remember, the key to successful scaling is building strong systems, hiring the right people, investing in their training, and making strategic outsourcing decisions. Stick to these principles, and you'll soon be operating a profitable, thriving business that not only meets but exceeds your clients' expectations.

Chapter 11. Financial Management: Pricing, Invoicing, and Regular Taxes

Essential ingredients of a ripe business strategy are sound financial management principles. Ensuring the right pricing, meticulous invoicing, and by-the-books taxation practice define a successful venture in many folds. So, let's discuss them in detail.

11.1. Determining Your Pricing Strategy

Creating a well-thought-out approach to your pricing strategy can indeed be a difference-maker for your business. Pricing services should not only make you feel fairly compensated but also perceived as a good value by clients.

Initially, explore your market. Get to know the average pricing for VA services, especially those that match your service offerings and skill set. Investigate by client industry, as well as by geographic location. Doing this initial legwork will help you determine a competitive baseline from which to start.

Consider basing your rates on the value provided to the client, instead of calculating based strictly on the time spent. This pricing model allows you to benefit from efficiencies you gain through experience and the use of cutting-edge tools.

Bear in mind that as you gain more skills and become more adept at productivity, your rates should reflect that. And ensure that you take into account all aspects of what it takes to run your business, including time spent marketing, communicating with clients and prospects, and administrative tasks.

11.2. Getting Paid: Ensuring Accurate and Timely Invoicing

Efficient invoicing is a vital part of maintaining a healthy cash flow in your VA business. Advances in technology have provided several excellent options for streamlining the invoicing process.

An invoice management system should enable you to quickly and easily generate invoices, issuing them promptly to avoid any delay in payment. Many accounting software packages come with invoicing tools. Some even allow for the creation of customized invoice templates, adding a professional touch.

Adding a polite payment due date or a gentle late-payment penalty clause can help you get paid on time. Understand your client's payment processes. Some companies might pay invoices once a month, and knowing this can save you unnecessary worry or surprise.

Digital payment options such as PayPal, Stripe, and others provide quick, easy, and reliable methods for clients to settle invoices. Some virtual assistants consider including their payment link directly in their digital invoices, which further streamlines the payment process.

11.3. Navigating the World of Taxes

Taxes can be the most complex aspect of running a virtual assistant business. However, understanding your tax obligations is critical.

If you are earning income as a virtual assistant, it's likely you are classified as self-employed, and therefore you have to manage your tax affairs diligently.

Tax laws vary by country, state, and even city, so you'll need to research what applies in your specific location. Track your business-related expenses religiously, as they will likely be deductible. This can range from a percentage of your home internet bill if you work from home, to office supplies, to subscriptions for business-related software.

It's also good practice to set aside a portion of your income for taxes. This will ensure you aren't caught unaware when it's time to file your returns.

In terms of VAT (Value Added Tax), if your earnings exceed a certain threshold - this amount varies by location - you will need to register for VAT. And, of course, you will need to factor this into your pricing structure.

Engaging a qualified tax professional can be invaluable. They can advise you on how to keep your books, what you can claim as expenses, and when and how to file your returns.

Remember, effective financial management is not just about making money, but also keeping it and growing it. By becoming proficient in pricing your services effectively, invoicing promptly and regularly, and managing your tax affairs effectively, you'll be setting your virtual assistant business up for long-term success. Implement these strategies, adjust when necessary, and the road to a profitable virtual assistant enterprise will look a lot less daunting.